A KING HELPS OUT

Prophet Muhammad for Little Hearts

by

SANIYASNAIN KHAN

Goodword**kidz**

Helping you build a family of faith

In 615 A.D., five years after the beginning of the revelation of the Quran, a group of the Prophet's Companions, weary of daily torture and hardship, left Makkah on the Prophet's advice to seek shelter in Abyssinia (Ethiopia) with the Christian ruler, King Najashi (Negus).

4

Under cover of nightfall 16 of them slipped away, to be followed later by another 83 men and women. When the Makkans discovered this, they were enraged, particularly because the children of many leading families were among them.

The Quraysh leaders sent two of their cleverest men to persuade King Najashi to send the Muslims back.

On arrival, they first gave gifts to the King's advisers, saying that some "foolish Makkans" had recently migrated to Abyssinia and that they intended to ask the king for their return.

8

Then they went to the King, and said, "Your Majesty, these people have abandoned the religion of Makkah, but they have not even become Christians like you." The King's advisers promptly urged him to hand them over straight away. But the King, unconvinced, became angry, saying, "No, by God, they came to me for protection and I will hear what they have to say."

The Makkans were dismayed at this, realizing that the King would immediately sense the migrants' sincerity. When the Muslims entered, they did not bow before King Najashi and were thereupon rebuked by the advisers. But the Muslims simply said, "We kneel only to Allah." Then King Najashi asked them about their religion.

13

The Muslims' spokesman, Ja'far ibn Abi Talib, 'Ali's brother and the Prophet's cousin, said: "O King, we and our ancestors turned away in ignorance from the faith of the Prophet Ibrahim (Abraham) عَلَيْهِ السَّلَام, who with Ismail (Ishmael) عَلَيْهِ السَّلَام, built the Kabah and worshipped only Allah. We did quite unspeakable things, worshipping idols, treating our neighbours unfairly, oppressing the weak and so on."

"This was our life until Allah sent a Messenger from among us, one of our own relatives, known always to have been honest, innocent and faithful. He asked us to worship only Allah, to give up the bad customs of our forefathers, to be truthful and trustworthy, to respect and help our neighbours, to honour our families and look after orphans, and to put an end to misdeeds and fighting. He ordered us to slander neither men nor women. He bade us worship none other than Allah, to pray, to give alms and to fast. We believe in him and follow his lead. The Makkans began to come between us and our religion, so we left our homes and came to you, hoping to find justice."

18

Hearing this, Najashi said, "Tell me some of the revelations which your Prophet claims to have received from God." Ja'far then recited some Quranic verses in which Maryam (Mary), the pure and devoted mother of the Prophet 'Isa (Jesus), has to face angry and disbelieving family members.

She points to the baby Isa ﷺ, but they say they cannot speak to a mere baby. Then Isa ﷺ himself astonishes them by uttering words of great wisdom.

Overwhelmed at this, the King exclaimed: "The messages of Jesus and Muhammad come from the same source!" And drawing a line with his cane on the floor, he said joyfully, "Between your religion and ours there is really no more difference than this line."

King Najashi gave the Muslims permission to live peacefully in his realm. The clever Makkans were sent home bitterly disappointed.